WILD SWIMMING
Log Book

Personal Information

Let's get started!

MY SWIMMING STUFF
(Don't forget anything!)

_____
_____
_____
_____
_____
_____
_____
_____
_____
_____
_____
_____
_____
_____
_____
_____
_____
_____

Date & Time:

Location:

Location details:

Parking:

Weather:

Air Temp:

Water Temp:

Hazards:

Currents:

Distance: Time:

Notes:

Overall Rating:

Date & Time:

Location:

Location details:

Parking:

Weather:

Air Temp:

Water Temp:

Hazards:

Currents:

Distance: Time:

Notes:

Overall Rating:

Date & Time:

Location:

Location details:

Parking:

Weather:

Air Temp:

Water Temp:

Hazards:

Currents:

Distance: Time:

Notes:

Overall Rating:

Date & Time:

Location:

Location details:

Parking:

Weather:

Air Temp:

Water Temp:

Hazards:

Currents:

Distance: Time:

Notes:

Overall Rating:

Date & Time:

Location:

Location details:

Parking:

Weather:

Air Temp:

Water Temp:

Hazards:

Currents:

Distance: Time:

Notes:

Overall Rating:

Date & Time:

Location:

Location details:

Parking:

Weather:

Air Temp:

Water Temp:

Hazards:

Currents:

Distance: Time:

Notes:

Overall Rating:

| Date & Time: |
| Location: |
| Location details: |
| |
| Parking: |

| Weather: |
| Air Temp: |
| Water Temp: |
| Hazards: |
| Currents: |

| Distance: Time: |

Notes:

| |
| |
| |
| |
| |

Overall Rating:

Date & Time:

Location:

Location details:

Parking:

Weather:

Air Temp:

Water Temp:

Hazards:

Currents:

Distance: Time:

Notes:

Overall Rating:

Date & Time:

Location:

Location details:

Parking:

Weather:

Air Temp:

Water Temp:

Hazards:

Currents:

Distance: Time:

Notes:

Overall Rating:

Date & Time:

Location:

Location details:

Parking:

Weather:

Air Temp:

Water Temp:

Hazards:

Currents:

Distance: Time:

Notes:

Overall Rating:

Date & Time:

Location:

Location details:

Parking:

Weather:

Air Temp:

Water Temp:

Hazards:

Currents:

Distance: Time:

Notes:

Overall Rating:

Date & Time:

Location:

Location details:

Parking:

Weather:

Air Temp:

Water Temp:

Hazards:

Currents:

Distance: Time:

Notes:

Overall Rating:

Date & Time:

Location:

Location details:

Parking:

Weather:

Air Temp:

Water Temp:

Hazards:

Currents:

Distance: Time:

Notes:

Overall Rating:

Date & Time:

Location:

Location details:

Parking:

Weather:

Air Temp:

Water Temp:

Hazards:

Currents:

Distance: Time:

Notes:

Overall Rating:

Date & Time:

Location:

Location details:

Parking:

Weather:

Air Temp:

Water Temp:

Hazards:

Currents:

Distance: Time:

Notes:

Overall Rating:

Date & Time:

Location:

Location details:

Parking:

Weather:

Air Temp:

Water Temp:

Hazards:

Currents:

Distance: Time:

Notes:

Overall Rating:

Date & Time:

Location:

Location details:

Parking:

Weather:

Air Temp:

Water Temp:

Hazards:

Currents:

Distance: Time:

Notes:

Overall Rating:

Date & Time:

Location:

Location details:

Parking:

Weather:

Air Temp:

Water Temp:

Hazards:

Currents:

Distance: Time:

Notes:

Overall Rating:

Date & Time:

Location:

Location details:

Parking:

Weather:

Air Temp:

Water Temp:

Hazards:

Currents:

Distance: Time:

Notes:

Overall Rating:

Date & Time:

Location:

Location details:

Parking:

Weather:

Air Temp:

Water Temp:

Hazards:

Currents:

Distance: Time:

Notes:

Overall Rating:

Date & Time:

Location:

Location details:

Parking:

Weather:

Air Temp:

Water Temp:

Hazards:

Currents:

Distance: Time:

Notes:

Overall Rating:

Date & Time:

Location:

Location details:

Parking:

Weather:

Air Temp:

Water Temp:

Hazards:

Currents:

Distance: Time:

Notes:

Overall Rating:

Date & Time:

Location:

Location details:

Parking:

Weather:

Air Temp:

Water Temp:

Hazards:

Currents:

Distance: Time:

Notes:

Overall Rating:

Date & Time:

Location:

Location details:

Parking:

Weather:

Air Temp:

Water Temp:

Hazards:

Currents:

Distance: Time:

Notes:

Overall Rating:

Date & Time:

Location:

Location details:

Parking:

Weather:

Air Temp:

Water Temp:

Hazards:

Currents:

Distance: Time:

Notes:

Overall Rating:

Date & Time:

Location:

Location details:

Parking:

Weather:

Air Temp:

Water Temp:

Hazards:

Currents:

Distance: Time:

Notes:

Overall Rating:

Date & Time:

Location:

Location details:

Parking:

Weather:

Air Temp:

Water Temp:

Hazards:

Currents:

Distance: Time:

Notes:

Overall Rating:

Date & Time:

Location:

Location details:

Parking:

Weather:

Air Temp:

Water Temp:

Hazards:

Currents:

Distance: Time:

Notes:

Overall Rating:

Date & Time:

Location:

Location details:

Parking:

Weather:

Air Temp:

Water Temp:

Hazards:

Currents:

Distance: Time:

Notes:

Overall Rating:

Date & Time:

Location:

Location details:

Parking:

Weather:

Air Temp:

Water Temp:

Hazards:

Currents:

Distance: Time:

Notes:

Overall Rating:

Date & Time:

Location:

Location details:

Parking:

Weather:

Air Temp:

Water Temp:

Hazards:

Currents:

Distance: Time:

Notes:

Overall Rating:

Date & Time:

Location:

Location details:

Parking:

Weather:

Air Temp:

Water Temp:

Hazards:

Currents:

Distance: Time:

Notes:

Overall Rating:

Date & Time:

Location:

Location details:

Parking:

Weather:

Air Temp:

Water Temp:

Hazards:

Currents:

Distance: Time:

Notes:

Overall Rating:

Date & Time:

Location:

Location details:

Parking:

Weather:

Air Temp:

Water Temp:

Hazards:

Currents:

Distance: Time:

Notes:

Overall Rating:

Date & Time:

Location:

Location details:

Parking:

Weather:

Air Temp:

Water Temp:

Hazards:

Currents:

Distance: Time:

Notes:

Overall Rating:

Date & Time:

Location:

Location details:

Parking:

Weather:

Air Temp:

Water Temp:

Hazards:

Currents:

Distance: Time:

Notes:

Overall Rating:

Date & Time:

Location:

Location details:

Parking:

Weather:

Air Temp:

Water Temp:

Hazards:

Currents:

Distance: Time:

Notes:

Overall Rating:

Date & Time:

Location:

Location details:

Parking:

Weather:

Air Temp:

Water Temp:

Hazards:

Currents:

Distance: Time:

Notes:

Overall Rating:

Date & Time:

Location:

Location details:

Parking:

Weather:

Air Temp:

Water Temp:

Hazards:

Currents:

Distance: Time:

Notes:

Overall Rating:

Date & Time:

Location:

Location details:

Parking:

Weather:

Air Temp:

Water Temp:

Hazards:

Currents:

Distance: Time:

Notes:

Overall Rating:

Date & Time:

Location:

Location details:

Parking:

Weather:

Air Temp:

Water Temp:

Hazards:

Currents:

Distance: Time:

Notes:

Overall Rating:

Date & Time:

Location:

Location details:

Parking:

Weather:

Air Temp:

Water Temp:

Hazards:

Currents:

Distance: Time:

Notes:

Overall Rating:

Date & Time:

Location:

Location details:

Parking:

Weather:

Air Temp:

Water Temp:

Hazards:

Currents:

Distance: Time:

Notes:

Overall Rating:

Date & Time:

Location:

Location details:

Parking:

Weather:

Air Temp:

Water Temp:

Hazards:

Currents:

Distance: Time:

Notes:

Overall Rating:

Date & Time:

Location:

Location details:

Parking:

Weather:

Air Temp:

Water Temp:

Hazards:

Currents:

Distance: Time:

Notes:

Overall Rating:

Date & Time:

Location:

Location details:

Parking:

Weather:

Air Temp:

Water Temp:

Hazards:

Currents:

Distance: Time:

Notes:

Overall Rating:

Date & Time:

Location:

Location details:

Parking:

Weather:

Air Temp:

Water Temp:

Hazards:

Currents:

Distance: Time:

Notes:

Overall Rating:

Date & Time:

Location:

Location details:

Parking:

Weather:

Air Temp:

Water Temp:

Hazards:

Currents:

Distance: Time:

Notes:

Overall Rating:

Date & Time:

Location:

Location details:

Parking:

Weather:

Air Temp:

Water Temp:

Hazards:

Currents:

Distance: Time:

Notes:

Overall Rating:

Date & Time:

Location:

Location details:

Parking:

Weather:

Air Temp:

Water Temp:

Hazards:

Currents:

Distance: Time:

Notes:

Overall Rating:

Date & Time:

Location:

Location details:

Parking:

Weather:

Air Temp:

Water Temp:

Hazards:

Currents:

Distance: Time:

Notes:

Overall Rating:

Date & Time:

Location:

Location details:

Parking:

Weather:

Air Temp:

Water Temp:

Hazards:

Currents:

Distance: Time:

Notes:

Overall Rating:

Date & Time:

Location:

Location details:

Parking:

Weather:

Air Temp:

Water Temp:

Hazards:

Currents:

Distance: Time:

Notes:

Overall Rating:

Date & Time:

Location:

Location details:

Parking:

Weather:

Air Temp:

Water Temp:

Hazards:

Currents:

Distance: Time:

Notes:

Overall Rating:

Date & Time:

Location:

Location details:

Parking:

Weather:

Air Temp:

Water Temp:

Hazards:

Currents:

Distance: Time:

Notes:

Overall Rating:

Date & Time:

Location:

Location details:

Parking:

Weather:

Air Temp:

Water Temp:

Hazards:

Currents:

Distance: Time:

Notes:

Overall Rating:

Date & Time:

Location:

Location details:

Parking:

Weather:

Air Temp:

Water Temp:

Hazards:

Currents:

Distance: Time:

Notes:

Overall Rating:

Date & Time:

Location:

Location details:

Parking:

Weather:

Air Temp:

Water Temp:

Hazards:

Currents:

Distance: Time:

Notes:

Overall Rating:

Date & Time:

Location:

Location details:

Parking:

Weather:

Air Temp:

Water Temp:

Hazards:

Currents:

Distance: Time:

Notes:

Overall Rating:

Date & Time:

Location:

Location details:

Parking:

Weather:

Air Temp:

Water Temp:

Hazards:

Currents:

Distance: Time:

Notes:

Overall Rating:

| Date & Time: |
| Location: |
| Location details: |
| |
| Parking: |

| Weather: |
| Air Temp: |
| Water Temp: |
| Hazards: |
| Currents: |

| Distance: Time: |

Notes:

| |
| |
| |
| |
| |
| |

Overall Rating:

Date & Time:

Location:

Location details:

Parking:

Weather:

Air Temp:

Water Temp:

Hazards:

Currents:

Distance: Time:

Notes:

Overall Rating:

Date & Time:

Location:

Location details:

Parking:

Weather:

Air Temp:

Water Temp:

Hazards:

Currents:

Distance: Time:

Notes:

Overall Rating:

Date & Time:

Location:

Location details:

Parking:

Weather:

Air Temp:

Water Temp:

Hazards:

Currents:

Distance: Time:

Notes:

Overall Rating:

Date & Time:

Location:

Location details:

Parking:

Weather:

Air Temp:

Water Temp:

Hazards:

Currents:

Distance: Time:

Notes:

Overall Rating:

Date & Time:

Location:

Location details:

Parking:

Weather:

Air Temp:

Water Temp:

Hazards:

Currents:

Distance: Time:

Notes:

Overall Rating:

Date & Time:

Location:

Location details:

Parking:

Weather:

Air Temp:

Water Temp:

Hazards:

Currents:

Distance: Time:

Notes:

Overall Rating:

Date & Time:

Location:

Location details:

Parking:

Weather:

Air Temp:

Water Temp:

Hazards:

Currents:

Distance: Time:

Notes:

Overall Rating:

Date & Time:

Location:

Location details:

Parking:

Weather:

Air Temp:

Water Temp:

Hazards:

Currents:

Distance: Time:

Notes:

Overall Rating:

Date & Time:

Location:

Location details:

Parking:

Weather:

Air Temp:

Water Temp:

Hazards:

Currents:

Distance: Time:

Notes:

Overall Rating:

Date & Time:

Location:

Location details:

Parking:

Weather:

Air Temp:

Water Temp:

Hazards:

Currents:

Distance: Time:

Notes:

Overall Rating:

Date & Time:

Location:

Location details:

Parking:

Weather:

Air Temp:

Water Temp:

Hazards:

Currents:

Distance: Time:

Notes:

Overall Rating:

| Date & Time: |
| Location: |
| Location details: |
| |
| Parking: |

| Weather: |
| Air Temp: |
| Water Temp: |
| Hazards: |
| Currents: |

| Distance: Time: |

Notes:

| |
| |
| |
| |
| |

Overall Rating:

Date & Time:

Location:

Location details:

Parking:

Weather:

Air Temp:

Water Temp:

Hazards:

Currents:

Distance: Time:

Notes:

Overall Rating:

Date & Time:

Location:

Location details:

Parking:

Weather:

Air Temp:

Water Temp:

Hazards:

Currents:

Distance: Time:

Notes:

Overall Rating:

Date & Time:

Location:

Location details:

Parking:

Weather:

Air Temp:

Water Temp:

Hazards:

Currents:

Distance: Time:

Notes:

Overall Rating:

Date & Time:

Location:

Location details:

Parking:

Weather:

Air Temp:

Water Temp:

Hazards:

Currents:

Distance: Time:

Notes:

Overall Rating:

Date & Time:

Location:

Location details:

Parking:

Weather:

Air Temp:

Water Temp:

Hazards:

Currents:

Distance: Time:

Notes:

Overall Rating:

Date & Time:

Location:

Location details:

Parking:

Weather:

Air Temp:

Water Temp:

Hazards:

Currents:

Distance: Time:

Notes:

Overall Rating:

Date & Time:

Location:

Location details:

Parking:

Weather:

Air Temp:

Water Temp:

Hazards:

Currents:

Distance: Time:

Notes:

Overall Rating:

Date & Time:

Location:

Location details:

Parking:

Weather:

Air Temp:

Water Temp:

Hazards:

Currents:

Distance: Time:

Notes:

Overall Rating:

Date & Time:

Location:

Location details:

Parking:

Weather:

Air Temp:

Water Temp:

Hazards:

Currents:

Distance: Time:

Notes:

Overall Rating:

Date & Time:

Location:

Location details:

Parking:

Weather:

Air Temp:

Water Temp:

Hazards:

Currents:

Distance: Time:

Notes:

Overall Rating:

Date & Time:

Location:

Location details:

Parking:

Weather:

Air Temp:

Water Temp:

Hazards:

Currents:

Distance: Time:

Notes:

Overall Rating:

Date & Time:

Location:

Location details:

Parking:

Weather:

Air Temp:

Water Temp:

Hazards:

Currents:

Distance: Time:

Notes:

Overall Rating:

Date & Time:

Location:

Location details:

Parking:

Weather:

Air Temp:

Water Temp:

Hazards:

Currents:

Distance: Time:

Notes:

Overall Rating:

Date & Time:

Location:

Location details:

Parking:

Weather:

Air Temp:

Water Temp:

Hazards:

Currents:

Distance: Time:

Notes:

Overall Rating:

Date & Time:

Location:

Location details:

Parking:

Weather:

Air Temp:

Water Temp:

Hazards:

Currents:

Distance: Time:

Notes:

Overall Rating:

Date & Time:

Location:

Location details:

Parking:

Weather:

Air Temp:

Water Temp:

Hazards:

Currents:

Distance: Time:

Notes:

Overall Rating:

Date & Time:

Location:

Location details:

Parking:

Weather:

Air Temp:

Water Temp:

Hazards:

Currents:

Distance: Time:

Notes:

Overall Rating:

Date & Time:

Location:

Location details:

Parking:

Weather:

Air Temp:

Water Temp:

Hazards:

Currents:

Distance: Time:

Notes:

Overall Rating:

Date & Time:

Location:

Location details:

Parking:

Weather:

Air Temp:

Water Temp:

Hazards:

Currents:

Distance: Time:

Notes:

Overall Rating:

Date & Time:

Location:

Location details:

Parking:

Weather:

Air Temp:

Water Temp:

Hazards:

Currents:

Distance: Time:

Notes:

Overall Rating:

Date & Time:

Location:

Location details:

Parking:

Weather:

Air Temp:

Water Temp:

Hazards:

Currents:

Distance: Time:

Notes:

Overall Rating:

Date & Time:

Location:

Location details:

Parking:

Weather:

Air Temp:

Water Temp:

Hazards:

Currents:

Distance: Time:

Notes:

Overall Rating:

Date & Time:

Location:

Location details:

Parking:

Weather:

Air Temp:

Water Temp:

Hazards:

Currents:

Distance: Time:

Notes:

Overall Rating:

Date & Time:

Location:

Location details:

Parking:

Weather:

Air Temp:

Water Temp:

Hazards:

Currents:

Distance: Time:

Notes:

Overall Rating:

Date & Time:

Location:

Location details:

Parking:

Weather:

Air Temp:

Water Temp:

Hazards:

Currents:

Distance: Time:

Notes:

Overall Rating:

Date & Time:

Location:

Location details:

Parking:

Weather:

Air Temp:

Water Temp:

Hazards:

Currents:

Distance: Time:

Notes:

Overall Rating:

Date & Time:

Location:

Location details:

Parking:

Weather:

Air Temp:

Water Temp:

Hazards:

Currents:

Distance: Time:

Notes:

Overall Rating:

Date & Time:

Location:

Location details:

Parking:

Weather:

Air Temp:

Water Temp:

Hazards:

Currents:

Distance: Time:

Notes:

Overall Rating:

Date & Time:

Location:

Location details:

Parking:

Weather:

Air Temp:

Water Temp:

Hazards:

Currents:

Distance: Time:

Notes:

Overall Rating:

Date & Time:

Location:

Location details:

Parking:

Weather:

Air Temp:

Water Temp:

Hazards:

Currents:

Distance: Time:

Notes:

Overall Rating:

Date & Time:

Location:

Location details:

Parking:

Weather:

Air Temp:

Water Temp:

Hazards:

Currents:

Distance: Time:

Notes:

Overall Rating:

Date & Time:

Location:

Location details:

Parking:

Weather:

Air Temp:

Water Temp:

Hazards:

Currents:

Distance: Time:

Notes:

Overall Rating:

Date & Time:

Location:

Location details:

Parking:

Weather:

Air Temp:

Water Temp:

Hazards:

Currents:

Distance: Time:

Notes:

Overall Rating:

Date & Time:

Location:

Location details:

Parking:

Weather:

Air Temp:

Water Temp:

Hazards:

Currents:

Distance: Time:

Notes:

Overall Rating:

Date & Time:

Location:

Location details:

Parking:

Weather:

Air Temp:

Water Temp:

Hazards:

Currents:

Distance: Time:

Notes:

Overall Rating:

Date & Time:
Location:
Location details:
Parking:

Weather:
Air Temp:
Water Temp:
Hazards:
Currents:

Distance: Time:

Notes:

Overall Rating:

Date & Time:

Location:

Location details:

Parking:

Weather:

Air Temp:

Water Temp:

Hazards:

Currents:

Distance: Time:

Notes:

Overall Rating:

NOTES & PHOTOS

NOTES & PHOTOS

NOTES & PHOTOS

NOTES & PHOTOS

NOTES & PHOTOS

NOTES & PHOTOS

NOTES & PHOTOS

RATE US!

Dear Customer,
Without your voice we don't exist. Please, support us and leave a honest review on Amazon.

PS: If you like this book and need more space to save your adventures, go to our author profile and check out other covers (or buy the same one!). You might also consider purchasing a copy as a gift for your friend!

Printed in Great Britain
by Amazon

14201831R10071